HORSES!

by
Kathy Wilmore

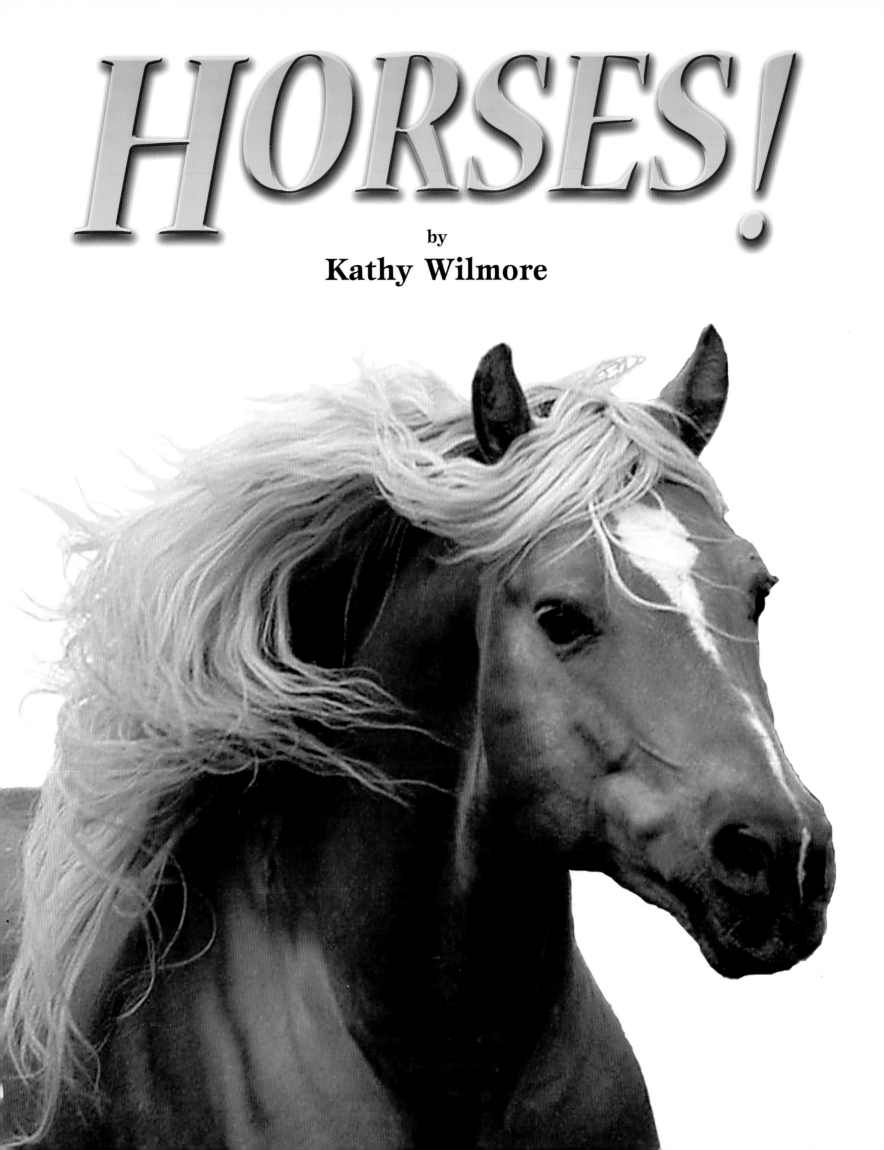

Picture Credits

AP Photo: pp. 39 *(top)*, 40-41 *(main)*

Kendra Bond: pp. 10, 11 *(main)*, 14-15 *(all)*, 16 *(bottom)*, 17 *(top)*, 22-23 *(center)*, 23 *(bottom)*, 32-33 *(center)*, 44-45 *(all)*

Alan & Sandy Carey: p. 7 *(main)*, 8-9 *(all)*, 16-17 *(center)*, 18, 22 *(left)*, 23 *(top)*, 26-27 *(main)*, 31 *(top)*, 43 *(top)*, 48

Comstock Images, Animals—Wildlife CD/comstock.com: pp. 4-5

Ron Kimball: pp. 18-19 *(center)*

Dwight Kuhn: p. 6

Dusty L. Perin: cover, pp. 26 *(left)*, 27 *(bottom)*, 28-29 *(all)*, 30-31 *(main)*, 32, 33 *(top)*, 34-35 *(all)*, 36-37 *(all)*, 39 *(bottom)*, 40 *(left)*, 41 *(right)*, 42-43 *(main)*, 43 *(right)*

Lynn M. Stone: pp. 13 *(top)*, 19 *(top right)*, 21 *(bottom)*, 24-25 *(main)*, 25 *(top)*, 30 *(left)*

Visuals Unlimited/Adam Jones: p. 24

Visuals Unlimited/Mark Newman: pp. 20-21 *(main)*

Visuals Unlimited/Inga Spencer: pp. 12-13 *(main)*

C. Jeanne White: p. 20 *(bottom)*

CONTENTS

INTRODUCTION

Horses are beautiful, powerful animals with very unique traits and a vast history. In this book, you will discover interesting information and facts on twenty popular types of horses. Through full-color photos and *Breed Basics*, you will learn all about the history, sizes, coloring, and other main characteristics of each one.

But before you saddle up, you should know the difference between a horse and a pony. The difference lies in the height, which is measured in *hands*.

In the world of horses, a hand is a unit of measurement used to describe the height of horses and ponies. One hand equals four inches. Horses and ponies are measured at the withers (the ridge between the shoulder bones). Ponies measure under 14.2 hands (56.8 inches) when fully grown. Horses stand over 14.2 hands when fully grown.

Now that you have that key knowledge under your belt, you are ready to ride into the wonderful world of horses and ponies.

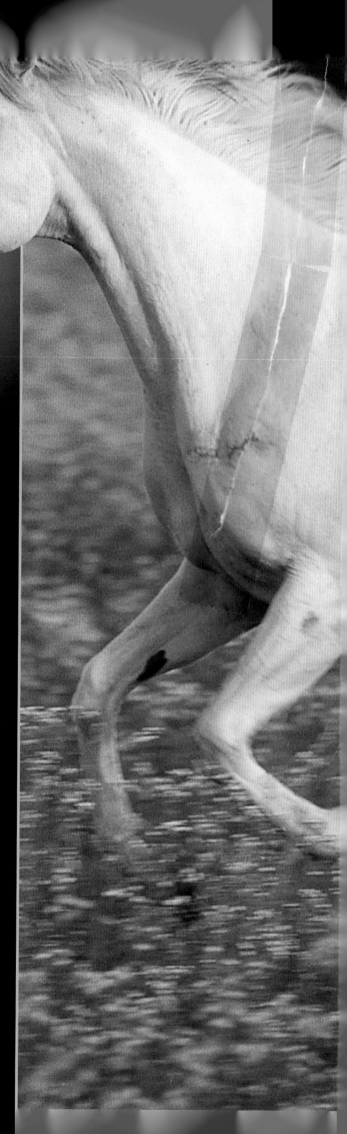

ARABIAN

A Long, Long Line

The Arabian is the oldest of all purebred horse lines. There is evidence that the breed existed on the Arabian peninsula as early as 2500 B.C. Most horse breeds today have at least some Arabian blood. This breed is admired as much for its courage and strength as for its beauty. People have ridden Arabians as warhorses and for long journeys across the desert.

▲ Starting Young

These gentle, affectionate animals are known for their spirit, intelligence, energy, and agile, graceful moves. This Arabian foal, just hours old, already shows those qualities, which have made its bloodline prized all over the world. While Arabians may be a variety of colors, including gray, brown, or black, they are most often reddish brown with white markings.

High-tailing It

This horse has long legs that are slim, but strong. A standard feature of this breed is its high-carried tail, as this mare *(below)* and her nursing foal show. The high tail comes from having fewer tailbones than other horses. Most Arabians have 16 tailbones and 22 vertebrae (backbones). Other breeds have 18 tailbones and 24 vertebrae.

BREED BASICS

Name: from the Arabian peninsula, where they were first bred
Date & place of origin: perhaps as far back as 2500 B.C., on the Arabian Peninsula
Usual height: 15 hands (60 inches)
Usual weight: 800 to 1,000 pounds
Main characteristics: a small head with large eyes; a long neck and short back; high, curving hindquarters; a long, silky mane and tail

PINTO

Who Spilled the Paint?

Pinto refers to a horse's coloring, not its breed. A pinto is a horse or pony with a coat of two different colors, in either of two distinctive patterns. The *overo (oh-VAIR-oh)* pinto pattern is large patches of white on a mostly dark-colored coat. The *tobiano (toh-bee-YAH-noh)* pinto pattern is large patches of color on a mostly white coat. The word *pinto* comes from *pintado (pin-TAH-doh)*, the Spanish word for "painted."

The pinto foal at left has an overo coat. Its companion's coat is tobiano.

Getting Official

Pintos can be found among many different breeds. There are official groups that help determine if a horse or pony is a pinto. They don't always agree. There is more than one set of rules used to classify a horse or pony as a pinto.

8

Color Schemes

Some people refer to pintos as either piebalds or skewbalds. The word *piebald* (PIE-bald) describes a pinto with white and black as its two coat colors. The pattern can be either overo or tobiano. *Skewbald* (SKYOO-bald) describes a pinto with a coat that is white and any color other than black, of either pattern. This pinto, for instance, is a *tobiano* skewbald.

BREED BASICS

Also known as: piebald, skewbald, particolored, or calico; some particular pinto breeds are known as paints

Date & place of origin: unknown; pinto denotes a coloring rather than a particular breed

Usual height: pinto horses, 14.2 to 16 hands (56.8 to 64 inches); pinto ponies, under 14.2 hands (56.8 inches)

Usual weight: depends on breed of the horse or pony

Main characteristics: a coat showing large areas of white and a dark color (usually black or brown); the mane and tail also may be of two colors

SHETLAND PONY

Packin' It In

Before being adopted as pets for children, Shetland ponies were put to work as packhorses in English coal mines. A mix of several British and Scandinavian breeds, the Shetland can be found in almost every coat color and pattern.

Best Buds

Beloved as pets, Shetlands make the perfect mounts for small children. They are gentle, patient, and willing to be trained. Shetland ponies—the smallest breed of horse—are the only horses not measured in hands.

Mighty Mites

The Shetland Islands of Scotland lie just 400 miles south of the Arctic Circle. That cold, rocky, extremely windy place is the original home of these animals. Tough enough to thrive there, Shetland ponies have been hard-working companions for the islands' farmers and fishermen.

The Shetland's strong, agile legs and thick coat, mane, and tail are important keys to its survival in the harsh climate of its homeland.

BREED BASICS

Name: from the Shetland Islands of Scotland; also, once known as pit ponies because they worked in coal mines

Date & place of origin: as far back as the Bronze Age (which began 4000 to 3000 B.C.), in Scotland's northern islands

Usual height: 40 inches (Shetlands are not measured in hands.)

Usual weight: about 300 pounds

Main characteristics: a small head with large eyes; a short, thick neck; and a long, thick mane and tail

11

MUSTANG

Wild Things

Mustangs are wild horses of the American West. They have run free for centuries, traveling in small, independent herds and defying efforts to tame them. These nomads are fierce, fleet, and sturdy. True mustangs descend from horses brought here by early Spanish explorers. Others descend from runaway ranch horses.

Catch 'em If You Can

Cowboys often rounded up mustangs and trained them to help herd cattle. They sometimes called an untamed mustang a bronco or bronc. Another name for this small, tough horse is cayuse *(KYE-yoose)*.

Staying Alive

Mustangs once roamed the plains in large numbers. A century ago, about one million ran free. Today, however, there may be fewer than 50,000 of these beautiful horses. Alarmed by this drop in number, many people are working to protect them. Some mustangs now live on reserve land. Others are rounded up for people to adopt.

BREED BASICS

Name: from the Mexican Spanish word *mestengo*, which means "stray"

Date & place of origin: the 16th century, in what is now Mexico and southwestern U.S.

Usual height: 14 hands (56 inches)

Usual weight: 800 pounds

Main characteristics: a small body, with a short neck; low withers (the space between a horse's shoulder blades); and low, sloping hindquarters

PALOMINO

Going for the Gold

Palomino is a coloring, not a breed. To be considered a palomino, a horse's coat must be evenly colored and within three shades (darker or lighter) of a newly minted gold coin. The mane and tail must be white or cream-colored. Only a few white markings on the face and legs are allowed, and the eyes must be black, brown, or hazel.

◄ Pretty as a Picture

A palomino's breed and temperament often determine how it is used. Some are used to herd cattle, and others run racecourses. The beauty of these horses also makes them popular mounts at riding stables and in parades, horse shows, and other on-display events.

▲ Jewel of the Crown

The popularity of palominos goes back centuries. During ancient times, these magnificent animals were ridden by emperors, kings, and queens.

BREED BASICS

Name: probably from the Spanish word for "dove" (*paloma*)

Date & place of origin: unknown; horses of this coloring are found all over the world and in many different breeds

Usual height: 14.1 to 16 hands (56.4 to 64 inches)

Usual weight: about 1,000 pounds

Main characteristics: an evenly-colored, golden coat with a white or cream-colored mane and tail; the only markings allowed are a white patch on the face and/or white on the lower legs

LIPIZZANER

Lookin' Good!

This regal-looking horse was first bred for one purpose: to look impressive. Members of the royal family of Europe's Austro-Hungarian Empire were the only people allowed to own or ride Lipizzaners (*lip-piz-ZAHN-erz*). The horses also pulled royal carriages.

BREED BASICS

Also known as: Lipizzan (*alternate spelling:* Lippizaner)

Date & place of origin: about 1580 in Lipizza, in what was then the Austro-Hungarian Empire (now Slovenia)

Usual height: 15 to 16.1 hands (60 to 64.4 inches)

Usual weight: 1,000 to 1,300 pounds

Main characteristics: a long head with a thick neck; long back; powerful body; and strong legs; born black or dark gray, but turns white by 7 to 10 years of age

Warhorse

Lipizzaner-related traditions, including the riders' uniforms, come from the days when Lipizzaner stallions were used as warhorses.

▲ Not Too Cool for School

Lipizzaners are the breed associated with the world-famous Spanish Riding School in Vienna, Austria. A horse learns to perform special moves, called Airs Above the Ground, through years of intensive training. These elegant moves include leaps, kicks, trots, and poses.

Lipizzaners are still bred where they originated—in Lipiça (Lipizza), Slovenia.

QUARTER HORSE

An Early American

The quarter horse—also known as the American quarter horse—is one of the oldest recognized horse breeds in North America. This horse is fast, tough, strong, and smart. Easily trained, it is prized by cowboys, cowgirls, and rodeo riders for its speed and its ability to make sudden stops, starts, and turns.

BREED BASICS

Name: from the quarter-mile stretches they ran as early American race horses; they became known as the "quarter-mile" or quarter horse
Date & place of origin: early 17th century, in the U.S.—a cross-breeding of horses brought by early Spanish settlers and horses brought by English settlers
Usual height: 14.3 to 16 hands (57.2 to 64 inches)
Usual weight: 950 to 1,200 pounds
Main characteristics: a broad, short head; thick neck and wide chest; stocky body; and muscular shoulders and legs

▼ Handy Companion

A solid, reddish-brown coat and a dark mane and tail describe their most common coloring, but quarter horses can be found in many colors. These strong, even-tempered horses have willingly performed many kinds of tasks: pulling plows and carriages, towing lumber, herding cattle, and exploring trails.

◄ Go West, Young Horse!

This horse is so fast over short distances that early English settlers in Rhode Island and Virginia used them as racehorses. When longer race courses became more popular, the Thoroughbred proved better for the job. However, quarter horses remained popular as trail and cow horses as the nation spread west.

CLYDESDALE

▲ On the Job

Clydesdales are draft horses—working horses that are hitched together to pull heavy carts or wagons. The Clydesdale is known for its high-stepping, springy gait, which comes from its large, powerful hindquarters and long, powerful legs. Its hard, flat hooves fare well on the pavement of city streets.

◄ Horse o' the World?

The Clydesdale originated in Scotland, and today is found throughout Scotland and northern England. There are some in North America, parts of Europe, South Africa, and Japan. They also can be found in New Zealand and Australia, where their hard work won them the nickname of "the breed that built Australia."

▲ The Clydesdale Look

Shaggy, silky hair on the lower legs is the most well-known Clydesdale trait. These young Clydesdales already show their breed's powerful shoulders and hindquarters. Working Clydesdales have regular tails. A show horse of this breed has a shaved, stubby tail that is decorated with ribbons.

BREED BASICS

Name: from the valley of the River Clyde in Scotland (the word *dale* means "valley")
Date & place of origin: 1715 to 1720, in Scotland
Usual height: 17 to 18 hands (68 to 72 inches)
Usual weight: 2,000 pounds
Main characteristics: a wide forehead; deep, thick body; large hindquarters; long hind legs; strong legs and feet; and long, silky hair on the lower legs

APPALOOSA

Spot On!

The most distinctive thing about this breed is its spotted coat. There are five Appaloosa coat patterns: blanket (a white or spotted area over the hips), frost (dark with white specks), leopard (white with dark oval spots), marble (a blotchy pattern over the whole body), and snowflake (white spots over the entire body).

▲ "Buffalo Horses"

The Nez Percé Indians admired these horses. They called Appaloosas "buffalo horses," because their speed, toughness, and courage made them a perfect ride for hunting buffalo.

On the Dot

Appaloosas come in many colors, but all have specks or blotches of contrasting color— from only over the hips or nose to over the entire body.

BREED BASICS

Name: from the Palouse River of Idaho and Washington

Date & place of origin: mid-1700s, first bred by the Nez Percé Indians in northwestern territories of the U.S.

Usual height: 14.2 to 16 hands (56.8 to 64 inches)

Usual weight: 1,000 to 1,100 pounds

Main characteristics: compact body; strong legs; the distinctive Appaloosa coat pattern; and tougher-than-usual hooves

Long Tradition

This young rider's costume honors the Nez Percé, who were among the greatest of Native American horse breeders, and who first bred the Appaloosa.

THOROUGHBRED

Born to Run

From the beginning, Thoroughbred horses were bred for one thing: racing. If you have ever watched the Kentucky Derby or any other major horse race, the horses you saw were Thoroughbreds. Another place you often see Thoroughbreds is at horse shows, where they jump hurdles and perform fancy moves known as dressage *(druh-SAHJ)*.

▲ All in the Family

Thoroughbreds were first bred in England from three types of horses: Byerly Turks, Darley Arabians, and Godolphin Arabians. Today these beautiful horses are bred in many countries around the world.

Purebred

Thoroughbred should not be confused with *purebred*. A Thoroughbred is a particular breed of horse. A purebred is a horse of any breed whose ancestors (all of the same breed) can be traced back several generations.

Go, Baby, Go!

Thoroughbreds can run faster than any other breed of horse. They run as fast as 45 miles per hour—even carrying a jockey weighing up to 115 pounds. Besides being fast, Thoroughbreds are exceptionally competitive, strong, and brave. However, they also tend to be nervous and sensitive. They must be raised, trained, and handled with care.

BREED BASICS

Also known as: English Thoroughbred
Date & place of origin: 17th century to 18th century England, bred (as racehorses) for power and speed
Usual height: 16 hands (64 inches)
Usual weight: 1,000 pounds
Main characteristics: a delicate, alert head with a long, graceful neck; strong, sloping shoulders; a long body; and long, fine-boned legs

ICELANDIC

No Strangers Allowed

The isolation of Iceland—this horse's native land—allowed the breed to remain pure for a thousand years. Although short enough to be considered ponies, Icelandics are always called horses in their homeland.

What *Can't* They Do?

The pride of Iceland, this breed is found in many ancient myths and tales. Today, people use them as workhorses, racehorses, show horses, riding horses, and pets. Some Icelandics still run wild.

A heavy coat and long, shaggy mane help this animal withstand Iceland's harsh Arctic climate.

There It Goes!

Icelandics are known for the *tölt* (*tuhlt*), a gait particular to the breed. A sort of running walk, the *tölt* enables Icelandics to easily maneuver rocky, uneven ground and deep snow. Icelandics also perform the tölt at horse shows and in races.

BREED BASICS

Name: from Iceland, the place where they have been bred for about 1,000 years

Date & place of origin: purebred since the 9th century, when their ancestors were taken to Iceland from Norway

Usual height: 12.3 to 13.1 hands (49.2 to 52.4 inches)

Usual weight: 800 to 1,000 pounds

Main characteristics: large head; long mane and tail; compact body; thick, heavy coat; and short, strong, shaggy legs; also, has an unusual gait called the *tölt* (a sort of running walk)

MARWARI

◄ Now Ear This!

The most distinctive feature of a Marwari is its curly ears. The Marwari probably descends from a mix of both tough desert horses of central Asia and Arabians. In the 12th century, horse breeders in the Marwar region of north-western India began raising them as a particular breed.

Who Needs a Camel?

The Marwari has long legs, a high-set body, strong ankles, and tough hooves. The angle of its shoulders keeps it from being a fast runner, but helps it walk well in sand. That, plus the fact that it can go long periods without water, makes it a good ride for desert dwellers.

▲ Tint Talk

Marwaris can be almost any color, but most are brown, reddish brown, or cream-colored, with blotches of white.

BREED BASICS

Name: from the Marwar region of India
Date & place of origin: unknown, but probably the 12th century, in northwestern India
Usual height: 14 to 15.2 hands (56 to 60.8 inches)
Usual weight: 800 to 1,000 pounds
Main characteristics: curling ears; long, flat forehead; deep, powerful chest and muscular body; long legs and strong ankles; extra-tough hooves

Man's Best Friend

Known for its courage, loyalty, and stamina, the Marwari was prized by warriors who rode it into battle during the late 16th and early 17th centuries. They knew that this horse would not shy away from loud noises or attacking enemies, and that it would stay and defend its rider if he fell.

BELGIAN HEAVY DRAFT

Get Out Your Map!

This horse is known by several names: Brabant, Belgian Heavy Draft, and Flanders horse. Each name points to this breed's place of origin. *Brabant* is a province in central Belgium. *Belgian Heavy Draft* refers to the horse's ability to pull heavy loads as well as to the place it was bred. Flanders was the medieval name for an area that included all of Belgium and parts of France and the Netherlands.

▲

Weatherproof Workhorse

Known as the "Great Horse" during medieval times (A.D. 900–1500), this powerful workhorse long earned its keep. A Belgian horse's great strength enables it to pull heavy loads, even through deep snow or mud.

Red, White, and No Blue

Belgians have been imported and bred in many places around the world, including Russia, Germany, Italy, France, and the U.S. In the U.S., the most common coloring is a coat that is chestnut (reddish brown) or roan (black, brown, or red hairs mixed with white), a white or pale yellow mane and tail, and white markings on the face and legs. However, it can be other colors as well, including light brown, dark orange, or even black.

BREED BASICS

Also known as: the Belgian Heavy Draft, Brabant, or Flanders horse

Date & place of origin: ancient times (100 B.C.); native to the part of western Europe that is now Belgium

Usual height: 16 to 18 hands (64 to 72 inches)

Usual weight: 1,800 to 2,200 pounds

Main characteristics: short, muscular neck and legs; broad, powerful chest; thick body; shaggy hair on legs above the hooves

31

MORGAN

Chips Off the Old Block

The original Morgan was a small horse named Figure, born in West Springfield, Massachusetts in 1789. Figure was surprisingly strong and fast for his size, which caught people's attention and admiration. People started calling him "the Justin Morgan horse," after his first owner, a Vermont schoolmaster. Figure's later owners bred him, starting the line known today as the Morgan breed.

Jack-of-All-Trades

Today's Morgans may not be as small as their ancestor, Figure, but they resemble him in many ways. Morgans are strong, fast, gentle, intelligent, and patient. The perfect multipurpose animal, they make excellent workhorses, are fine for riding, and also participate in horse shows and races.

Justin Morgan, All-American

Morgans are the oldest breed of horse originating in the United States. The original Justin Morgan horse was a bay—its coat was reddish brown with black markings. Bay coloring is still common among this breed, but you also will find Morgans that are black, brown, chestnut (reddish brown), cream-colored, gray, or palomino.

BREED BASICS

Name: from Justin Morgan, a schoolmaster who owned the horse from which other Morgan horses were bred

Date & place of origin: about 1789, in West Springfield, Massachusetts

Usual height: 14.1 to 15.2 hands (56.4 to 60.8 inches)

Usual weight: 900 to 1,100 pounds

Main characteristics: bright, expressive eyes; head held upright; muscular back and hindquarters; strong, slender legs; and long tail

PASO FINO

A Real Pal

Paso Finos are lively, smart, and affectionate horses, often on the small side. This makes them popular as show horses, trail horses, and as mounts for beginning riders. These peppy, eager-to-please animals come in every color and pattern.

▲ On With the Show

Paso fino is Spanish for "fine step"—fine, in this case, meaning "very small." Paso Fino show horses perform three special gaits: *paso fino* (fine step), *paso corto* (short step), and *paso largo* (long step).

BREED BASICS

Name: from their gait; *paso fino* is Spanish for "fine step"

Date & place of origin: 16th century; descended from horses brought to the Americas by early Spanish explorers

Usual height: 13 to 15.2 hands (52 to 60.8 inches)

Usual weight: 800 to 1,200 pounds

Main characteristics: large, expressive eyes; short neck; muscular chest; long, strong, and flexible hind legs; and long mane and tail

▲ Old-Timers

This horse descends from the first horses in the western hemisphere, which were brought to the Americas by Spanish explorers. These horses were mixed with later-arriving breeds, eventually branching into new breeds, including the Paso Fino.

HAFLINGER

Made for the Mountains

The Haflinger, which originated in the Tyrol (*tuh-ROLE*) region of Europe's Alps, is not afraid of steep terrain. Whether running free or towing a heavy load, the Haflinger gets power from its muscular chest and legs. Haflingers raised high in the Alps also develop larger hearts and lungs, which help them keep going in harsh conditions.

▲ Care for a Trim?

The Haflinger's trademark pale mane and tail are long—though not always as long as those of this Haflinger stallion!

Shady Characters

You won't see a wide variety of coat colors and patterns among Haflingers. Many are palomino, though some have coats in lighter or darker shades of reddish brown.

◄ Live Long and Prosper

Haflingers can be found in many parts of the world. They are welcomed for their even temperament, willingness to work, and eagerness to please. Often used as draft horses, packhorses, and trail horses, Haflingers work long and hard—for 30 years or more.

BREED BASICS

Name: from the town of Hafling (once Austria, now part of Italy)

Date & place of origin: about 1874 in the Tyrol region of the Alps

Usual height: 13.1 to 15 hands (52.4 to 60 inches)

Usual weight: 800 to 1,200 pounds

Main characteristics: coat color ranging from pale palomino to dark chestnut; long, pale mane and tail; broad chest; a long, strong back; muscular legs; and tough, hardy hooves

CHINCOTEAGUE

In the Mix

These hardy ponies are born in the wild on the Chincoteague *(SHING-kuh-teeg)* and Assateague *(AH-suh-teeg)* islands off Maryland and Virginia. They are a mix of many horse and pony breeds, including Welsh, Shetland, mustang, Barb, and Arabian. Parts of their native islands are now protected national wildlife areas where about 200 ponies still roam free.

▲ Splish-Splash!

Every summer, these ponies go for a big swim. Guided by herders, they cross the bay from their islands to the mainland. There, young ones are sold, tamed, and raised—often as riding horses or pets for children. This event was made famous by a hugely popular children's book, *Misty of Chincoteague* by Marguerite Henry.

▲ Going Wild

According to a popular legend, the ponies first reached the islands by swimming ashore after a 16th-century shipwreck. That probably isn't true. They most likely were abandoned by early settlers, or strayed from the mainland in the 17th century. No matter how they got there, they grew tough and wild on the salty, marshy islands.

BREED BASICS

Name: from one of the islands off the Maryland and Virginia coasts, where they live in the wild

Date & place of origin: late 17th century, when they found their way onto the islands (stories of how they got there vary)

Usual height: 12 to 13 hands (48 to 52 inches)

Usual weight: 600 to 700 pounds

Main characteristics: broad forehead; small ears; short back; fine-boned legs; widely varied coloring, with pinto patterns common

AMERICAN STANDARDBRED

Specialty Horse

These horses are bred with one purpose in mind: harness racing. First known as trotters, most American Standardbreds are excellent pacers (meaning that they move at a fast, two-beat gait). In harness, the earliest racers of this breed could cover a mile in three minutes.

Today's American Standardbreds often cover the same distance in under two minutes!

They Get Around

American Standardbreds are calmer than their Thoroughbred ancestors. Their easy-going nature makes them good riding horses after they retire from racing. They also are favored as cart and carriage horses by the Amish, whose religious beliefs do not allow them to drive cars.

▼ It's in the Genes

The ancestor of all Standardbreds—Hambletonian 10—had a swift trotting style. His great-grandfather was a Thoroughbred named Messenger, a fine trotting horse brought to the U.S. in 1788. For 20 years, Messenger was bred with various kinds of mares. He never raced in the U.S., but he had raced in England. His swift trotting style, passed on to Hambletonian 10, is a key characteristic of all American Standardbreds.

BREED BASICS

Name: from the standard trotting speed horses once had to reach on a mile-long course to be registered to this breed

Date & place of origin: 1849, when Hambletonian 10, ancestor of all American Standardbreds, was born in Orange County, New York

Usual height: 15 to 16 hands (60 to 64 inches)

Usual weight: 800 to 1,000 pounds

Main characteristics: long, low body; strong muscles in the upper front legs; powerful hindquarters; and tough, level hooves

AMERICAN SADDLEBRED

Step Right Up!

Popular as a horse-show competitor, this horse is known as either a three-gaited or a five-gaited horse. The three gaits are walking, trotting, and cantering (slowly galloping). The five gaits are the first three, plus the slow gait and the rack (a rapid, four-beat movement). The American Saddlebred's characteristic high step comes naturally, but trainers reinforce it by putting weights on the hooves during training.

General Appeal

This spirited breed, known as a comfortable ride, was the favorite mount of 19th-century plantation owners and Civil War generals. In fact, the well-known horse of Robert E. Lee, the South's most-famous general, was an American Saddlebred named Traveller. Traveller was gray with black markings, but this breed may have any coat color or pattern.

Put Me In, Coach!

This horse is at ease jumping hurdles and strutting its stuff, which is why it is so often seen at shows. Its speed, strength, and willingness to learn have made it a good candidate for many other activities, including hunting, towing plows or carriages, herding cattle, navigating trails, and pleasure riding.

BREED BASICS

Also known as: American Saddle Horse
Date & place of origin: early 1800s in the U.S., with Kentucky the foremost breeding place; first recognized as a separate breed in 1891
Usual height: 15 to 17 hands (60 to 68 inches)
Usual weight: 1,000 to 1,200 pounds
Main characteristics: long, arched neck; muscular hindquarters; long, slender legs; springy, high-stepping gaits

WELSH

Welsh Section A,
also called the Welsh
Mountain Pony

Starting Small

At one time, these ponies ran wild or were used as workhorses in the mines of Wales. Today, they are popular as pets. Breeders divide Welsh ponies into four groups: Sections A, B, C, and D. The original, called the Welsh Mountain Pony (Section A), is the smallest of the four.

Welsh Section B, also
called the Welsh pony

B Is for "Best in Show"

The Section B Welsh is a little larger than the original Welsh Mountain Pony. For generations, it was used by farmers to pull carts and herd livestock. Strong, smart, and even-tempered, the Welsh Pony is a good mount for children learning to ride. It is an excellent jumper, and does very well as a show horse.

▼ A Couple of Cobs ▶

The two Cob-type animals in the Welsh family are a mix of Welsh Mountain ponies, Spanish ponies, and horses taken to Wales by ancient Romans. They are called Cobs because of their stocky, short-legged bodies.

Welsh Section C, also called the Welsh Pony of Cob type

BREED BASICS

Names (four types): Welsh Mountain Pony, Welsh Pony, Welsh Pony of Cob Type, and Welsh Cob

Date & place of origin: ancient times, in Wales (the original Welsh Mountain ponies)

Usual height: A—up to 12 hands (48 inches); B & C—up to 13.2 hands (52.8 inches); D—up to 15 hands (60 inches)

Usual weight: about 500 to 900 pounds

Main characteristics: variations on the Welsh Mountain Pony's small head, pointed ears, wide forehead, and high-carried tail

Welsh Section D, also called the Welsh Cob. C-type Cobs are small enough to be called ponies, but the larger D types are considered horses.

GLOSSARY

bay: a red to brown coat with black points (Points are the mane, tail, ear tips, muzzle, and lower legs.)

bloodline: an unbroken series of direct ancestors (such as parent, grandparent, great-grandparent, and so on)

breed: *noun*—a group of animals with similar characteristics, usually having common ancestors

breed: *verb*—to control the type of offspring by matching males and females with particular characteristics

bronc or bronco: an untamed mustang

canter: a three-beat gait that is a little slower and smoother than a gallop

chestnut: a reddish-brown coat, usually with legs and ears all the same color

draft horse: a horse that is able to pull heavy loads

foal: a young horse or pony, especially one that is under one year in age (A colt is a young male horse; a filly is a young female horse.)

gait: a horse's style or manner of foot movement, including walk, trot, pace, canter, or gallop

gallop: a horse's fastest natural gait—a rapid, bouncy, three-beat gait

hand: a unit of measurement equal to four inches, used to describe horses and ponies

overo: large patches of white on a coat that is mostly a solid color; one of two distinctive pinto coat patterns

pace: a fast, two-beat gait

pacer: a horse that excels in pacing (moving with a fast, two-beat gait)

purebred: a horse whose ancestors can be traced back several generations, and were all of the same breed

roan: a dark-colored coat (such as brown or black) that looks lighter because many white hairs are mixed in

tobiano: large patches of color on a coat that is mostly white; one of two distinctive pinto coats

trot: a somewhat quick gait that is somewhere between a walk and a gallop

trotter: a horse that excels in trotting